SWEET, YOUNG, & WORRIED

SWEET, YOUNG, & WORRIED

poems by Blythe Baird

Button Publishing Inc.
Minneapolis
2022

SWEET, YOUNG, & WORRIED

◇

Published by Button Poetry / Exploding Pinecone Press
Minneapolis, MN 55403 | http://www.buttonpoetry.com

◇

All Rights Reserved
Manufactured in the United States of America
Cover design: Talisa Almonte
ISBN 978-1-63834-049-2
26 25 24 23 22   1 2 3 4 5

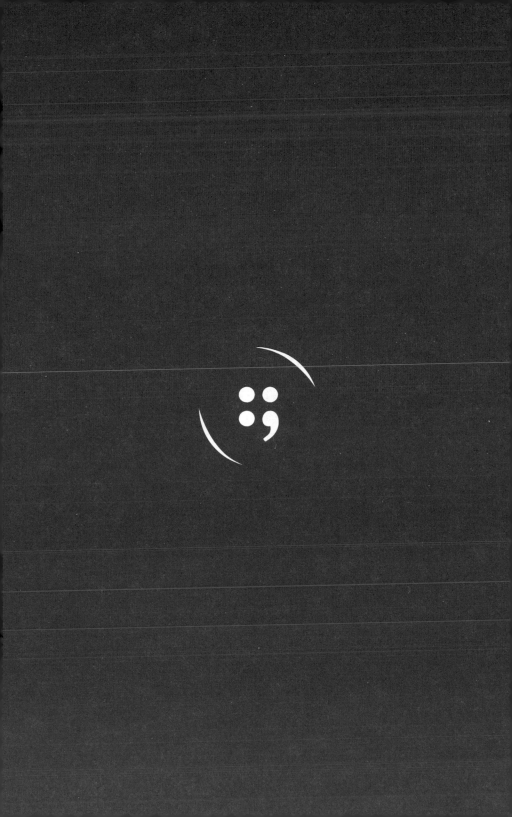

"*Sweet, Young, & Worried* immediately captures the reader and does not let us go lightly. With great control, Baird ushers us through the landscape of youth and suffering with her usual palpable imagery and haunting narratives. This book is a homecoming of sorts; it brings us back to ourselves."

—SIERRA DEMULDER

CONTENTS

iii. A PLACE WE HAVEN'T BEEN TO YET

TO BECOME AN EMERGENCY

part one

"Even now, I don't know much
about happiness. I still worry
and want an endless stream of more,
but some days I can see the point
in growing something, even if
it's just to say I cared enough."

—*ADA LIMÓN*

IN THE SHAPE OF A POEM

This is an
apology

to all of
the wounds

I locked
in the cellar

of myself

to punish them
for refusing

to heal

in the shape
of a poem.

SAD GIRLS CLUB

we protected our sadnesses
like they were our most talented

children. and perhaps we were
just proud of ourselves

for managing to keep something
alive, even if it was our own pain.

so, we kept getting straight A's.
we kept sneaking out to pierce

each other's cartilages with dirty
push pins on dark playgrounds.

we kept pressing tiny perforated
clippings of white blotting paper

on top of our tongues. we
slept with pea-sized capsules

underneath our mattresses
like pulseless princesses.

we were sweet sixteen and
starving all week; passing

out in the bathroom stall
at the junior year prom.

I am worried about all of us.
we swear nothing is wrong.

we were just scratching
our wrists! and biting our
nails! and throwing up!

we already told you;
we're not hungry.

we don't want your
stupid granola bar.

at home, we dissolved
diet pills in diet Dr. Peppers.

fake fruit rotted on
the kitchen counter.

it is one thing
to want help

and another

to have the
language

to ask for it.

in the meantime,
we were getting high

in someone's garage;

giggling about
swallowing

bleach.

we joked about
suicide so often

it became difficult to tell
the difference between

a punchline
and a promise.

we scorched the cold metal
of our mental illnesses until

they softened together
into sparkling silver

charms on our
friendship bracelets.

we didn't know what to do
with the shame that we felt

for our tragedies, but we did
know how to structure a shrine
made of them. I wonder where

we learned to worship that?

I mean, we were thirteen
the first time we logged

on to www.tumblr.com
on the family desktop,

photos of birthday cakes
with the words *I WANT*

TO DIE spelled out in
cocaine cursive frosting.

we watched looping
black and white clips

of blades ice skating
against swollen wrists.

we saw that screenshot
of that girl from *Skins*

captioned with something
about how she didn't eat

for three days so she could
be lovely, and suddenly

all everyone I know
wants to be is *lovely*.

so, we lined the edges
of our self-destruction
with lavender linens.

we watched chain links
of daisies spill from mouths
of bedazzled shotguns.

we spent hours
devouring

#thinspiration
and #sadgirlsclub.

how does anybody heal
in a culture that glorifies

self-hate? beyond that,
how does a *teenager*

heal in a culture that
glorifies self-hate?

the internet told us
that we mattered

when we suffered,
assured us we were still
pretty when we cried,

but what we heard

is that crying
is what made us

pretty,

and suffering
is what made us

matter.

so, when the walls
of ourselves

finally did cave in,

we decided to unpack
our things and live

in this amethyst-
encrusted debris.

what if someone
had told us that

we didn't
have to

be bleeding

in order
to be open?

what if someone
had told me

that a wound was
not the only way

to travel into
the center

of myself?

THE NIGHTS I FELT IRIDESCENT

do whatever
you can

to avoid making
your sadness

into your
aesthetic.

if you attach
too much

of your
identity

to melancholy,
it will be

that much
harder

to learn
your worth

as something
that lies outside

the barrier
of your suffering.

you do not
have to be

a catastrophe
to prove

you are worth
paying attention to.

I am still pacing
the halls of myself.

why did I not
allow myself

to clutch the
shooting stars

of my happiness

as tightly as the
dissolving sea

of my grief?

why is there so
little evidence

of all the nights
I felt iridescent?

why am I clawing
through a haystack

of old feelings
just to find

a needle of my
delight?

I still don't
know how

to write about
the things that

didn't
hurt.

WHAT A BODY INHERITS
after Hieu Minh Nguyen

My mother is the only person
who has ever hated my body

more than I do.

The full moon of my belly
hanging over the lip of my jeans

mortified me,
I mean—*us.*

I remember sitting cross-
legged on the bathroom floor

while she put on makeup;
her sighs littering the vanity.

She looks in the mirror
the same way I look

at a scale, all before photo—sucked
gut—never unnoticeable enough.

My mother catches her reflection
in a store window and I hollow out

my cheeks. She pinches a wad
of flesh from her lower back

and my tailbone stiffens.
I gain twenty pounds

and my mother
becomes a migraine.

She confesses that sometimes
she truly believes she is hideous

and I apologize.

I'll admit: I blamed her
for teaching me how

to be cruel to my body
because she let me

watch her set fire
to her own.

My poor mother.
She didn't think I was

paying attention.
It isn't her fault

that she didn't notice
the missing rolls

of measuring tape.
She didn't realize

I was taking notes.

I need you to know
it is easy to blame

a memory; to gossip
about a woman

who cannot tell her
side of the story

as long as she is
a character

I can prop up like a doll
in my retelling of it.

When she complains
that she never wanted

to be something for me to
write about, I roll my eyes.

I yank the yarn from her smile
until she has no mouth.

My poor mother. I cannot let
anything be her fault, even if

it was. Especially if it was.
Because if it was, I have to

acknowledge that I
have never bothered

to ask my mother
why she is unhappy.

If I invite her to give
her endless well

of grief
a name,

I am afraid
it will be

mine.

BLOW POP DIET

the boys stayed up late
playing strip-tac-toe

with metallic sharpies on our
strawberry lemonade cheeks.

we couldn't hold our liquor
because we never ate dinner.

we got banned from the local
hookah lounge—the joint that

once named flavor combinations
after us—not for being underage

but because too many of us
fainted when we stood up.

trading after school wasn't
anything out of the ordinary

until our pencil cases
full of silly bandz

got swapped out with
backpacks of ex-lax.

we cut peanut m&m's with a
white plastic knife, chewing

the candy-coated chocolate,
spitting mush into napkins

while the lunch ladies
shared wrinkled frowns.

there was once a rumor that
our whole friend group

survived exclusively on
blow pops & blow jobs,

& when we heard this,
we blushed & broke

out into laughing hyenas,
chins hitting the carpet

so everyone could see our teeth
splashed with phone-book yellows

our mouths tie-dyed cherry,
green apple, & blue raspberry—

whole rainbows clogged
in school bathroom sinks.

HOW TO BECOME A DISNEY CHANNEL ORIGINAL STAR

is the exact title of a diary entry I penned
at age 12. At the very top of the list was

Lose 30+ pounds!!! in sixth grade hand-
writing, highlighted and double underlined.

The year *Camp Rock* debuted, I wedged my front teeth
apart with metal pliers to get a gap like Demi Lovato's.

I presented my mom with clip art of clothing items
printed out from DressLikeDemi.com. I begged her to

take me to the Wet Seal at the mall. I was in the market
for a whole new look: I'm talking fedoras. Traffic cone

colored skinny jeans. Button-up mini vests. Vials of black
crackle nail polish. Suspenders with shoelace-thin straps.

Every morning, after straightening my hair to uncooked
spaghetti, I pressed the crescent moon of my thumbnail

into the center of my chin in an effort to dent a permanent
cleft into my skin. I plastered my bedroom with their face,

often cutting the Jonas Brothers out to make room for more
Demi-devoted wall space. I could not acknowledge my lust

for them, so I repackaged my emotions. I poured all my
energy into becoming synonymous with Demi Lovato.

I aspired to deteriorate in the same ways they did because
I hoped this would bring me closer to understanding them.

If I made them into my role model, there was no way they
could be my crush. I channeled the surges of hate I had for

myself into an unrequited obsession for my favorite celeb.
I loved them so deeply that I wanted to morph into them,

and the only way I knew how to relate to their pain
was by attempting to recreate it. The only grief I still

carry hits me when I hear how others first figured it out:
the barbarically beheaded Ken dolls, the life-size Barbies

they pretended to walk down aisles with, the realization
following the scene where Shego tackles Kim Possible,

Lindsay Lohan in every scene of *Herbie: Fully Loaded.*
I don't have a moment like this. Instead, I have pinhole

memories of etching "stay" and "strong" into my wrists
with a jagged paperclip, practicing my autograph in the

margins of my treatment plan notebook, so desperately
trying to dot my i's with the same Sharpie heart as Demi,

while the internalized homophobia I swallowed like gum
sunk deeper and deeper towards the floor of my stomach.

CAST LIST

in junior high school, it was so
imperative for me to be liked

that I conjured a gospel
out of the theater girls.

I watched the way the tenors
followed them out of choir

& the whole orchestra pit
gnawed on the bone of

their attention. I wanted
to be included so badly

that I was content with being
the reason for the slaughter

of their pitch-perfect laughter
as long as I was cool enough

to be getting off at
the same bus stop

as the most
popular girl

when she finally got
to the punchline.

MULTICOLORED PILLS

you are 15 when the multicolored
pills jumble together in your mouth
like a ball pit at a children's party.
you remember what came after in
dull snapshots: your sister using
a bobby pin to unlock your door,
finding you strewn across the bed
like a ragdoll. your slippery pulse.
shallow breath. a gurney with hard
cloth straps. a stiff paper gown with
visible creases from where it was
once neatly folded. the frantic hum
permeating the intensive care unit.
the needy DJ of beeping equipment.
you know something is not working.
you are handed a thick milkshake
of black activated liquid charcoal
in a styrofoam cup and a red straw.
it tastes like a mcflurry blended
with asphalt and sidewalk chalk.
your throat coats in thick layers of
tar. no one lets you have any water.
you splash night skies of black vomit
onto the walls and your father's polo
shirt. you are concerned that you have
ruined his shirt. after that, you sleep
for a long time. when you wake up,
the first thing you search for is a mirror.
you are concerned that you look ugly.

a sensible nurse fashions your hair
into a loose fishtail. she holds your
hand while she whispers sharply,

listen to me, kid.

your overdose
was near fatal.

there is nothing ugly
about you surviving

after we had to
tell your family

that you
may not.

CODE T14.91

The only way
I knew how

to acquire
attention

was to
become

an emergency.

        So, yes—

I waved
my arms

on an empty
runway

until my
shoulders

snapped out
of their

sockets.

Of course,
the plane had

no choice
but to land

at my
feet.

HOSPITAL HIGH SCHOOL

the dry crumbles of nature valley granola bars
kicked under vinyl grey chairs. green and yellow

foil wrappers folded into impressively mini cubes
before they were shoved between squeaky seats.

once a week, we had planned visits with our assigned
psychiatrist, psychologist, case manager, and parents.

these meetings were held in bright, sun-soaked offices
with free coffee and healthy plants in clay artisan pots.

when the parents were not there, our therapy sessions
occurred in blank rooms with no windows, illuminated

by migraine-waiting-to-happen fluorescent white over-
head lights. we sat in a crescent as a medical assistant

passed out red and white striped plastic bendy straws.
he instructed us to breathe through them as an exercise

designed to mimic a panic attack until a couple of us were
escorted out once the activity induced real panic attacks.

my friendships were a miscellaneous group:

a Katy Perry lookalike whose boyfriend
just committed suicide, a lesbian goth,
a shy girl with so much cystic acne
that it was painful to wear glasses,

a compassionate preteen boy who had to cover
his baby brother's eyes when the knife block
went missing and they rushed upstairs to find
their father bludgeoning their stepmom to death.

we were all encouraged to share the gory details
of our traumas (however, they forbade us from touch—
so after you did break down, no one could hug you.)

we pawed at lunch with peers who understood
what it is like to have cobwebs crawl your skull.
we talked about our anxieties and were met with
true support, empathy, and the kind of validation

that only self-identified fucked up teenagers can
provide fellow self-identified fucked up teenagers.

we were so used to being made into a mockery
until suddenly we found ourselves in a community.
it was everything we dreamed high school to be
except locked in the psych ward of a mental hospital.

we spoke in code of the holy depression we were

experiencing over our monitored fruit snack breaks
about jewelry and oral sex and Kardashian gossip

and the tongues our mothers bit and the sins
we don't get why our fathers won't just admit

and the frustration of how no one in "the real world"
seemed like they were ready to talk about any of this.

THE SCALE WAS THE LAST TO GO

because the first time you relapsed,
it was as if a director yelled *CUT!*

and just like that, the familiar set
of the bathroom was torn down

and replaced with
an awards show.

the tile floor shattered.
paparazzi crawled out
of the beige grout.

the towel left in a heap
on the floor stretched into
a terry cloth red carpet.

the viewers at home are dying
to know your secret. as if the

shortcut was as simple as
the first night you listened

to Fiona Apple sing, *hunger
hurts / but starving works,*

her voice filling you up
like flat soda and vinegar.

COME HOME, STOCKHOLM

oh, how humbling
it is to know:

the body
I threw stones at

is the same
body who is

still determined
to write

love letters
to me.

SKINNY GIRL MIRAGE

your eating
disorder

is never
going

to be able
to give you

whatever
the fuck it is

that you are
actually

looking for.

I PROMISE

the most
miserable

moments

of my
treatment

were still
sweeter

than the
greatest

moments

of my
sickness.

GUILTY BYSTANDER

do I still

have an

eating

disorder

if I didn't

eat

today

but

I didn't

torment

the rolls

piling up

on my

stomach,

either?

DRESS REHEARSAL

do I still have an

eating disorder

if I can prove

I ate everything

I was supposed

to eat today,

but I was

screeching

from the

stage wings

at my body

the entire time

like she forgot

her only line

in the script?

WHAT IF I CARED FOR MY BODY

half as much

as I care about
my poetry?

what if I cared
for myself

half as much
as I care about

what people
think of me?

what if,
when I finally

figure out
who I am,

I can't
stand her?

harder
to imagine:

what if
I loved her?

SPLINTERS OF IMPROVEMENT

part two

"Just a week ago, an opera singer
held her baby on her lap
as a mountain chewed their plane

to bits. How is that possible?
Didn't the mountain see the baby?"

— MAGGIE SMITH

THIS MUST BE ENOUGH

most of the time,
everything I do

is simply an attempt
to resent myself

more gently

and to cherish
myself more

violently.

GUILT DOESN'T LIVE HERE ANYMORE

you made it
through, girl.

you made it through
every single time

the world scratched
& skidded to an end.

you woke up. tomorrow
shoved you out of bed.

sure, some days the only
productive thing you did

was breathe, but even
when survival feels

like a performance,
it is still an art form.

staying alive is a skill
& you are so talented,

you sweet girl. you are
worth so much more

than sent emails &
crossed off to-do lists.

find victory in the small
things: the folded laundry,

the clean plate, the
answered phone call,

the brushed teeth.
you used to say

you were sorry every
other sentence, girl.

& now people tell you
that you make them feel

powerful

& you always
somehow forget

the fact that you dragged
yourself out of quicksand,

girl. you took notes
on the beauty

& the lessons
you gathered

while you
were sinking.

you escaped

the padlocked
jaw of shame

& when those
barbarian boys

pushed you over
the lip of the ship,

you were all
sucker-punch

& *bitch, I keep*
a life raft

in my smile.

I keep switchblades
in my mascara.

the next time
a motherfucker

comes knocking at
the door of my body

without an
invitation,

I'm gonna slice off
each of his fingers
like baby carrots.

I'm gonna drown him
in a boiling hot spring

of me toos.

I'm going to take
over the world

in spite of
everything

that has been done
to me & my body.

in fact, I'm going to
take over the world

because of everything

that has been done
to me & my body.

I am sharpening
my voice

into a sword.

I am becoming
a girl made

of mace.

I left hell
so I could

come back
& tell you

all about it,
& you know

what
I learned?

every time

I thought
my life was

ending,
turns out,

it was just
opening.

one day, the urge
to write a poem

became greater
than the urge

to write

a suicide
note.

and so,

I wrote
the poem.

WHAT TO EXPECT WHEN YOU ARE NOT

1.

I didn't need any help from
a fanny-packed protestor,

their swarms like a family
of gnats in front of the clinic.

I had already found thousands of
my own creatively nuclear ways

to ringlead the circus
of my shame.

2.

I have known I've wanted
to be an incredible mother

for as long as I have feared
being a regrettable daughter.

So, when the nurse
asked if I wanted

to see the sonogram,
I said *yes, please.*

I chose to give the crumb

on that matte black monitor

the most beautiful
name I could think of.

3.

When I get up from
the operation bed,

I am embarrassed that I've
dripped fat marbles of blood

onto the linoleum
floor. I am crying,

frantically reaching for
a roll of paper towels.

I try to clean
it up myself

until the gentle nurse
shoos my hand away.

*It's not your job
to fix it, honey.*

4.

But it feels like it is

my job to fix it,

honey.

5.

When she leaves the
room to let me change
out of my paper gown,

I cannot help myself
from peering into the
plastic blue bin labeled

*CAUTION. HAZARDOUS
WASTE. DO NOT OPEN.*

I was looking for another
reason to punish myself,

but inside the bin I found
only neatly bagged trash.

6.

For the next three years,
I kept the *What to Expect*

When You're Expecting
app on my phone. I chose to
receive the notifications.

I chose to know exactly
when my baby would

be the size of a poppy seed.
An apple seed. A sweet pea.
A blueberry. A raspberry.

A green olive. A kumquat.
A lime. A plum. A lemon.
A fat tomato. An avocado.

A pear. A bell pepper.
An artichoke by now.

7.

I chose to walk past
the newborn section of
Target again & again.

I chose to hold
a little Velcro gym shoe
in my hand.

I chose to fit my thumb
into a tiny cotton sock.

8.

I have never felt
entitled to grieve this.

I am scared of being called out
for how I can be unwaveringly

pro-choice,

yet still somehow have
a mobile of regrets

circling the crib above
my own decisions.

9.

If you were
wondering,

my baby would have
been a Libra

on the cusp
of nothing—

sure of himself
in a way

I could never
teach myself

how
to be.

THE ALGORITHM

I am flashing back
to the day
of the procedure:

Sierra gingerly
reminding me
of all the women

who have fought
and died

for my right to make
this decision.

Filling out a form
where I have to list
three reasons why

I am sure I want to go
through with this.

Chavah stealthily ripping
their Juul in the doctor's office,

cool mint vapor rushing
down their shirt collar.

The long wait for the nurse to
come back. Debating if we would
forgive Jordyn (if we were Kylie.)

Soon enough, my baby is right there
on the screen: so small & electronic & gone
that I could barely even catch a glimpse.

It was like trying to catch
the reflection of a sequin.

In the waiting room before the anti-
anxiety meds kick in, I get a ping
from one of those scrabble apps:

> Blythe, your word of the day
> is MOTHERHOOD.

I imagine drowning the device
in the bathroom sink. I am sick

of my phone knowing me like
a nosy friend. A volunteer asks
if I want to color a page of boobs
while I wait, which I think is

bizarre. I eat all of the silver
Hershey's Kisses on her desk.

She gives me a DIY bouquet
of condoms on my way out

tied together with
a rubber band bow.

I accept them politely
and without screaming.

HOLOGRAM OF A NURSERY

an app showed me

what he'd look like

when I touch his smile

my hand thuds into

his pixelated cheek

I stare at the mother

I refused to become

until the greenery

of my jealousy

wraps vines of

umbilical cords

around un-mother's

ghostly neck

you are the best

dream I have

ever followed,

she whispers

into my never-

son's ear,

and a glitch

of moonlight

spills ivory

across his face

until he looks

directly

at me

and suddenly

nothing

like me

NIGHTMARE IN WHICH PLANNED PARENTHOOD OPERATES OFF OF MY DINING ROOM TABLE

In it, I was
the doctor

performing
my own

abortion
procedure.

When the infant—
then no larger

than a Lego—

came out of me alive,
I hid the small body

in the freezer.

When I returned to
make sure he was

dead,

my baby was
all grown up—

a man

of identical size
to a coffin.

WHAT WOULD IT LOOK LIKE IF YOU FORGAVE YOURSELF?

My therapist

wants to know,

but we only have

six minutes left

in our session.

I silently show her

a swollen photograph

of a Good Mother—

a *Great* one, even—

but neither of us

can make out

whose.

TELEPHONE

your suburb smelt of burnt hair
and acrylic nails masqueraded

by a fog of citrus febreze.
once, under a jungle gym,

you found lipstick smeared on
the silicone mouth of a pacifier.

before you became the tightrope of
string shuttling messages between

the two tin cans of your parents,
you were a child. before you were

a child, you were a chip
of glass carefully wedged

into the palm of a marriage.
you didn't mind. every kid

who grew up as a splinter
understands. not everyone

is lucky enough to be born
surrounded by something.

SHOW AND TELL

My big sister and I bruise
easier than summer peaches.

We compare the purpling
sienna sunsets on our thighs

between schoolgirl snickers,
marveling at each other's
temporary blood tattoos.

At the pediatrician,
my sister gets a shot
and I cry because I am

jealous. I cry because
I want a good reason

to choke my mother's
hand and shriek, too.
Our mother says it isn't
ladylike for us to be

so obsessed with open
wounds. Sometimes,
we mistake our mother
for an open wound.

My sister and I are both
obsessed with her, too.

TAKING MY MOTHER TO A GAY BAR

After my college graduation,
my family is on the way
to celebrate at my favorite bar.

Everything is going
surprisingly well until someone
decides to interject,

Hey, Mom, you do know that the
Kitty Cat Klub is a gay bar, right?

Ok, fine, it was me. I interjected!
I guess I was just hoping

that when I told my mother we were
on our way to a gay bar, she would . . .

I don't know.
Surprise me?

Instead, my mother accidentally
throws a tantrum instead of a party.

You guys taking me here is
the equivalent of you throwing me
into a cage of hungry lions!

she howls. & it is not that I am
offended by her statement, but I am

afraid that this is how
she thinks of my love:

feral and bloodthirsty,
a glass room
of snapping mouths

baring sets of steak knives for
teeth, prowling, preparing to
pounce. In the car, she refuses to

look at me. Still, in this
moment, I do not cry.

My mother fumes. She displays
her anger like a centerpiece

at a supper table:
bold and purposeful.

The rest of my family awkwardly
scolds her, each of them bracing

for the clap of femme thunder
that they all expect from me,

but I just laugh.
I remind my mother

that not every episode

has to be a soap opera.

When we finally arrive at the
Kitty Cat Klub, it is still daylight.

My mother's dropped jaw drags
across the floor, collecting lint.
The bar is a pleasant ghost town.

*I want to leave when the gays
get here,* she complains.

In my mind, I respond: but
where will you go, Mom?

If I retrace every step
in my life to the very
beginning, you are

the *only* place
I always end up.

In real life, I say
nothing.

Because what am I
supposed to say?

*No, Mom, actually
it's too late for you*

to leave when the gays get here
because I'm literally right

here. You know that,
right? That I'm still here?

I have become the queen of
brushing off others' judgements,

even if doing so has
turned me

into a girl made of
dust.

Just don't let anybody touch me,
she sneers, her voice

more mousetrap
than mouth.

Later that night, I make a point
to hug her extra hard.

I do not cry because I love my mom.

I love my mom, though I am afraid
my sexuality will always be a bullet

point on the long list
of things about me

that my mother is
disgusted by.

I do not cry because
I have done that before,

and it did not make
anything softer.

In spite and as a result of
everything, I am *proud*

of my mother because
there was a very real time

in my life she would never,
under any circumstance,

have stepped foot into a gay
anything at all, so I tell her,

Thank you for coming here.
It means the world to me.

Because my mom
means the world

to me. And for her,
this was progress.

For me, the fact

that she came—

and even more so,
the fact that she *stayed*—

was a gift.

So, I will celebrate these
splinters of improvement.
I will take what I can get.

For my own well-being,
I have to acknowledge

that maybe,
in her world,

this really is the best
that my mom can do.

I love all of her, even if
there are aspects of myself

she still has no desire
to learn how to love.

Once, when I was
in high school,

we got in a fight so
merciless that even

the hardwood
floor cracked

under the pressure
to be spotless.

To calm down,

I thought of
how she cared

for the house
I grew up in

like it was her
favorite child:

the tender way
she would fluff

the pillows
on the sofa,

the meticulous way
she'd scrub and scrub
the countertops

until each one
became

a mirror.

I tell myself:

this is proof
that she cares

about
something.

It doesn't always
have to be

me.

SLEEPOVER IN A DIORAMA

your paper friends sit on small benches
of Jenga blocks praising your
cloudy homemade soup of hot glue.

thimble stew. they marvel at your talent
for keeping artificial succulents alive

and your collection
of homemade bouncy balls

constructed from the ends
of foot-long hotdogs.

more importantly: they carefully
shake hands with the flimsy parents
you cut out of print advertisements.

they were empathetic enough
to let you keep a small handful
of pretend truths for yourself.

you were once just a child
on a leash disguised
as a koala-shaped backpack.

and just look at you now:

hanging out with kids your
own age at a slumber party!

your true friends knew the shoebox
belonged to your actual mother—

the one who does not
have agates for eyes—

but they did not dare accuse you
of snipping her oversized grin
from recycled construction paper.

they kindly pretended
not to notice

the strips of scotch tape
holding her teeth

into place.

A SIGN SHE IS TRYING

When my best friend was a child,
her mother used *The Game of Life*
as a metaphor to explain sexuality.

You can have two pink guys or two
blue guys, you know, she would say.

My best friend is so straight,
she doesn't even masturbate.

Still, she always knew that
even if she wasn't, even if

someday she did end up shotgun
to another pink piece,

she knows she'd remain
loved and supported.

She would never
have to ask

for forgiveness.

Of all the things this world
has taught her to apologize for,

I am jealous that love has
never been one of them.

But last week, my mother
folded up her old flannels

and placed them
at the foot of my bed.

I know this is probably
just a coincidence—

not a peace treaty
or an attempt

to understand me—

but for my own well-being,
I have to take this as a sign

she is trying,
even if it isn't.

Even if she isn't.

A PLACE WE HAVEN'T
BEEN TO YET

part three

"In a study on love,
baby monkeys were given a choice
between a wire mother with milk
and a wool mother with none. Like them,
I would choose to starve and hold the soft body."

—ROBIN BETH SCHAER

DOME OF BUTTERFLIES

on our first date, we visit
a dome of butterflies.

outside the entrance,
a bright sign reads:

PLEASE DO NOT TOUCH
THE BUTTERFLIES!

LET THEM
LAND ON YOU!

same, I whisper to myself.
this is my love language:

please do not touch me.
please let me land on you.

GEM AND I

that summer, we slept on a navy hammock in the bee garden
& ripped pink bongs out of sephora bags under an ivy canopy
of emerald trees. we nicknamed our classmates after pokémon
& unfolded plastic lawn chairs to sit and watch the blood moon
clot. we sketched a catalogue of wild midwestern mushrooms
& sipped pouches of sweet vodka limeade until our tongues
pickled into something worth sharing. you lifted your peach dress
& offered me the red grid of fresh cuts on your upper thighs.
i painted yellow sunflowers over your soon-to-be scars, sweetly
& gently, until the acrylics began to sting your skin. we charged
your crystal collection under the clipped fingernail of a grey moon
& spoke nothing of the ways we have both tried to claw ourselves out
of our bodies. instead, we sang only of the joys, the pastel weekends,
& the good things that must live in a place we haven't been to yet.

GARDEN OF POETRY

I have been to this garden so many times,
the cherry blossom trees know my name.

Before it became a parking garage, this is where
I wrote & bellowed my first drafts to an audience

of shrubbery & wildflowers & the curved spines
of lavender. I hold a pen in one hand & the last

good news you gave to me in the other. I ask
for nothing & the wind whisks into applause.

I do not bring anyone here who I do not love.
It has become sacred to me, this quiet pocket
that feels like it is mine in this city that isn't

yet. On our walk, you are staring at the moths
& I am staring at you. I am in the middle of

another one of my stories, something my mom
told me about seeds—did I already tell you
about her green thumb? I can't remember now.

What I do remember is how you pointed
up toward the entrance as we came in.

Like a frantic canary, your voice is singing,
Look. Look! & out of all the dozens of times

I have been here, not once have I ever bothered
to glance up. Now, when I do, I see a steel arch
towering high above our heads with the words

GARDEN OF POETRY stretched
in block letters the size of textbooks.

Later, we are sitting on a bench
outside. You open your mouth

& the cicadas stop
shrieking to listen.

My fingers are wrapped
around a tuft of weeds

that I am just about to
yank from the ground

but you stop my hand

mid-air,

      shouting, *No, don't—*
      that's a bellflower!

& suddenly

this plant I nearly murdered
in my palm a mere moment ago

became beautiful
& worth preserving

simply because
you told me

it was.

TO LOVE AN ARTIST

it is difficult

for an artist
to fall in love

with another
artist.

we are both
trying

to capture
the other.

we both
desperately

want the
other

to hold

still.

BELLE OF THE RAVE

— danced like the flame of a sparked candle
pastel lavender hair flickering in the sharp
whip of the stage fans and electric drums

— glittered her way through the crowd
with her glassy eyes and spaceship grin
the high of hating yourself delicately

— dressed in a jewelry scale ball gown
for the e-cigarette shop after-party and
dehydrated teens and dilated pupils

— weaved her way through the strobing lights
and the massage trains and dirty mattresses
and the neon body paint and the Ziploc bags

— winked at the couple with the candy dripping
from their wrists who kept chanting at us
in the empty parking lot: *KISS! KISS! KISS!*

— stepped on an injured bird in heels and kept
walking because I never stopped you

(and I never told you)
so, you never looked down

so, you never noticed
  that it was there

    or that now   it is dead.

MY POWER

after another
unrequited love

leaves me

with dandelions
wilting

in my fists,

I sigh to Sierra
about how I hope

I stop feeling
everything

so intensely
when I get older.

well, I hope you
never stop feeling

things so
intensely,

she responds.
that is

your power.

ENDLING

You cannot
endanger me.

I will keep
channeling

Hydra,

the many-
headed

serpent.

For every
one of

her heads
that gets

severed,

two new,
deadlier

skulls
spawn

rapidly
in its
place.

THE MOST USELESS EMOTION

There is a close relationship between people
& fear. If anyone sees something that may

    be dangerous, we erupt with the lazy feeling
    of homesickness. I am hypnotized by being

young & fiercely inconvenienced
by logic. Most of all, I fear trying

    to bring something important to the world
    & failing. It is not difficult to welcome havoc,

to fall in love with a storm
named after a girl or a girl

    named after a flower. We enjoy discussing
    death & going out to dive bars & dancing.

We obsess over shame (the most
useless emotion I can think of).

    My primary reason for not keeping a rifle is that I would
    like to shoot the snakes, the prey, the late swollen nights

a boy cupped me tightly in his hands like I was a fire

fly or some other small, bright, trappable thing.

    I would say I am not much of a hunter myself,
    but then again, my memory is not what it used

to be. Oftentimes, I find
myself in a place

        too familiar to bother
        panicking, although

knowing this has
yet to stop me.

AFTER THE POETRY SLAM IS OVER

you will still be

significant

    & intelligent

    & worthwhile

    & creative

    & lovable

    & talented

        & brave

        & alive

        & forgiven

        & allowed

           to be happy

              even if you never

pry open the portal

of your wounds

with the crowbar

of your writing

ever again.

TO DEVOUR A SKY

most moments

    would devour

        a sky

    or a symphony

          as trivial

      as time

      but here—

soft glass rose

from a greenhouse

of a girl &

the summer let go

of my silk   dress

do you still like

to swim

in funnel

clouds

& dance

on pink

sheets   of ice?

please sit here

        with me

        & remember:

we were sweet

        & young

& worrying

        -ly brilliant.

ACKNOWLEDGEMENTS

Many of these poems would not exist without the funding of a 2020 artists fellowship awarded by The McKnight Foundation and The Loft Literary Center. I am also perpetually grateful for Bao Phi, Arleta Little, Jenny Dodgson, and every single one of my Loft Literary Center students.

Thank you to Sam, Tanesha, Riley, and the Button Poetry team for reassuring me that people still care about what I have to say.

Thank you to my managers at Management by Morgan, Lisa and Joe.

Thank you to Sierra DeMulder and Siaara Freeman; the best mentors a girl could ever ask for.

Thank you to HB and Nash for sticking with me for over a decade; for growing with me simultaneously yet in different directions. Thank you for sharing your mothers with me.

Thank you to Donte Collins, my cherished best friend. Thank you for being my favorite place to come home to. I could recognize your laugh from miles away. I will have your back until the end of time.

Thank you to Jessie, my big sister, role model, and soon-to-be most loving mom on the planet.

Thank you to my littlest love, who doesn't yet exist but will by the time this book debuts. I can't wait to meet you, my Taurean niece.

Thank you to Ben, Andrea, Travis, my mom, and my dad.

Thank you to my dazzling, supportive, wildly incredible friends: Fatima, Ladan, Chavah, Mary Beth Becker-Lauth, Brenna, Margret, Robert, Presley, Bailee, Topaz, Miss Mari, and Corbin.

Thank you to the Chicago Slam Scene that built me: Kwabena, Mojdeh, Billy, Raych, Toaster, Nate, Eric, and Adrienne. Thank you. to Young Chicago Authors, Lethal Poetry, and Louder Than A Bomb.

Thank you to anyone who has held my work against their chest, wrapped themselves in it, who both kept it safe and shared it with others, who has written to me with their own stories, who has whispered a stanza aloud in a quiet room just for the comfort of it. I appreciate you. Thank you for caring about my truths and experiences and observations. Thank you for teaching me about yours. Thank you for allowing me to see you. Thank you for the gift of being seen. I love you.

BIRTHCHART

Name		Sign		House	Deg	Name		Sign		Deg
	Sun		Leo	8	13.7°	Ascendant		Sagittarius	18.3°
	Moon		Taurus	5	9.8°	House 2		Capricorn	24°
	Mercury		Virgo	9	6.6°	House 3		Pisces	4.7°
	Venus		Gemini	7	28.9°	House 4		Aries	10.4°
	Mars		Cancer	7	7.4°	House 5		Taurus	7.6°
	Jupiter		Capricorn	1	9.1°	House 6		Taurus	29.1°
	Saturn		Aries	3	7.1°	House 7		Gemini	18.3°
	Uranus		Aquarius	2	2.1°	House 8		Cancer	24°
	Neptune		Capricorn	2	25.9°	House 9		Virgo	4.7°
	Pluto		Sagittarius	12	0.3°	MC		Libra	10.4°
☊	North Node		Libra	9	9.7°	House 11		Scorpio	7.6°
⚸	Lilith		Leo	8	4.9°	House 12		Scorpio	29.1°

ABOUT THE AUTHOR

At only 25 years old, Blythe Baird is already one of the most recognizable and acclaimed names in spoken word poetry.

Originally from the northwest suburbs of Chicago, the viral writer has garnered international recognition for her stunning performance pieces that speak urgently and honestly about sexual assault, mental illness, eating disorder recovery, sexuality, and healing from trauma.

Her work has been featured by *Glamour*, *ELLE*, TEDxMinneapolis, The National Eating Disorder Association, *Mic*, *The Huffington Post*, Everyday Feminism, Medium, The Mighty, *The Body Is Not an Apology*, Write Bloody, Button Poetry, A-Plus, and many more.

Baird graduated from Hamline University in 2018 with a dual degree in creative writing and women's studies. In 2020, she became the recipient of the prestigious McKnight Artist Fellowship for Spoken Word administered by The Loft Literary Center in Minnesota.

OTHER BOOKS BY BUTTON POETRY

If you enjoyed this book, please consider checking out some of our others, below. Readers like you allow us to keep broadcasting and publishing. Thank you!

Desireé Dallagiacomo, *SINK*
Dave Harris, *Patricide*
Michael Lee, *The Only Worlds We Know*
Raych Jackson, *Even the Saints Audition*
Brenna Twohy, *Swallowtail*
Porsha Olayiwola, *i shimmer sometimes, too*
Jared Singer, *Forgive Yourself These Tiny Acts of Self-Destruction*
Adam Falkner, *The Willies*
George Abraham, *Birthright*
Omar Holmon, *We Were All Someone Else Yesterday*
Rachel Wiley, *Fat Girl Finishing School*
Bianca Phipps, *crown noble*
Natasha T. Miller, *Butcher*
Kevin Kantor, *Please Come Off-Book*
Ollie Schminkey, *Dead Dad Jokes*
Reagan Myers, *Afterwards*
L.E. Bowman, *What I Learned From the Trees*
Patrick Roche, *A Socially Acceptable Breakdown*
Rachel Wiley, *Revenge Body*
Ebony Stewart, *BloodFresh*
Ebony Stewart, *Home.Girl.Hood.*
Kyle Tran Mhyre, *Not A Lot of Reasons to Sing, but Enough*
Steven Willis, *A Peculiar People*
Topaz Winters, *So, Stranger*
Siaara Freeman, *Urbanshee*
Junious "Jay" Ward, *Composition*
Darius Simpson, *Never Catch Me*

Available at buttonpoetry.com/shop and more!

FORTHCOMING BOOKS BY BUTTON POETRY

Robert Wood Lynn, *How to Maintain Eye Contact*
Mwende "FreeQuency" Katwiwa, *Becoming//Black*
Usman Hameedi, *We Plan On Staying Right Here*
Matt Mason, *Rock Stars*
Anita Dias, *Sitcom Material*

BUTTON BEST SELLERS

Neil Hilborn, *Our Numbered Days*
Hanif Abdurraqib, *The Crown Ain't Worth Much*
Sabrina Benaim, *Depression & Other Magic Tricks*
Rudy Francisco, *Helium*
Rachel Wiley, *Nothing Is Okay*
Neil Hilborn, *The Future*
Phil Kaye, *Date & Time*
Andrea Gibson, *Lord of the Butterflies*
Blythe Baird, *If My Body Could Speak*
Andrea Gibson, *You Better Be Lightning*

Available at buttonpoetry.com/shop and more!